Hummus, Haircuts, and Henna Parties

Creative Ways to Reach Out to Muslims

By Fouad Masri

Published by:

Crescent Project
P.O. Box 50986
Indianapolis, IN 46250

www.crescentproject.org

ISBN: 978-0-9843632-0-9

Printed in the United States of America.

Table of Contents

Step 1 – Finding a Muslim Friend...................... 3

Step 2 – Initiating a Relationship...................... 7

Step 3 – Deepening the Friendship................... 11

Step 4 – Meeting Felt Needs of Muslims............ 15

International Students and Immigrants......16

Women... 17

Families... 18

Step 5 – Asking Good Questions...................... 21

Step 6 – Sharing your Faith............................23

Preface

"I don't want to say the wrong thing." "What if he's a terrorist?" "If she's wearing a veil, would she want to talk to me?" "Will they be in danger if I tell them about Christ?"

I've heard comments like these many times over the years. Because of differences in religious practices, dress, and other customs, Christians are often hesitant to build relationships, or even just initiate conversations, with Muslims.

For too long, Christians have not been engaging with the Muslims in their communities. Andrea, after making a new friend from Bangladesh, was told that she was the first American friend she had in ten years of living in the U.S. Ten years! I'm so glad you've decided to play a part in turning this around.

This guide will help you to initiate friendships with Muslims, deepen them, and create opportunities to share the hope of Christ.

Don't be overwhelmed by the number of ideas. You don't need to read through each idea one by one. Instead, use these ideas to begin thinking creatively and strategically about how you can build deeper relationships. Be excited and expectant as God leads you in your interaction with Muslims in your community!

God has called the Church to share Christ with the world! The Great Commission is clear – the Good News of Jesus Christ is for *all* peoples. Are you ready to get engaged with Muslims around you?

– Fouad Masri

Step 1: Finding a Muslim Friend

Set a regular time to pray for Muslims.
A possible time to pray is at noon on Fridays, when Muslims are going to the mosque for Friday prayers. Pray for the Holy Spirit to open your eyes to the needs of Muslims in your city. (If you aren't currently subscribed to Call to Prayer, Crescent Project's bi-weekly email prayer bulletin, you can sign up at www.crescentproject.org/prayer.)

Visit local, Muslim-owned restaurants and businesses regularly.
Search for Muslim names in the Yellow Pages or on the Internet to discover the wonderful cultural experiences available nearby. Restaurants with Middle Eastern, Pakistani, Mediterranean, Somali, and often Indian cuisine are likely to have Muslim employees and patrons. If you haven't had hummus yet, you're in for a real treat.

Visit religious web sites and chat rooms.
Many Muslims are uninformed and need to learn from understanding Christians who display love, compassion, and tact. Sometimes you can begin conversations and connect with Muslims in chat rooms or Facebook groups.

Help the hurting.
Muslim refugees from across the globe have fled their homelands' wars and turmoil. Local agencies and non-profit organizations need volunteers to assist these families in their transition to life in North America.

Volunteering

One of my teammates heard that Muslim women were visiting the local Pregnancy Resource Center. So she went through the volunteer training program. At the first workshop she taught, seven of the twelve women were Muslims!

After having wonderful opportunities with these women, the Center informed her that she was not allowed to visit the clients' homes or have them over to her house. She was disappointed, but prayed that God would make a way.

God answered her prayers quickly. Two women, who my team member had connected with, graduated from the program.

They've since been able to visit several times and these relationships are beginning to develop.

Befriend the lonely.
Many international students are Muslims. Holidays can be a very lonely time, so it's a great opportunity to invite them over!

Befriend people who have converted to Islam from Christianity.
Learn why they converted. Your friendship can counteract inaccurate Biblical understanding or a negative opinion of Christians.

Visit your local mosque or Islamic center.
The mosque is a place where the Islamic community gathers. Call ahead to let them know you are a Christian and interested in learning more about what Muslims believe. You will likely be warmly received. When you go, be sure to take a friend, and pray silently throughout your entire visit. (Check out www.crescentproject.org/mosquevisit before you go.)

Outreach Packs

Crescent Project believes that we have a hope in Jesus that is worth sharing with all people. As a gift to Muslim immigrants and refugees, we have designed a gift pack of resources explaining why Jesus died to cover our sin and shame and why the New Testament has not been changed. It also includes the "JESUS" film, a movie on the life of Christ in several of the major languages that are spoken in the Muslim world.

Many believers have shared these Outreach Packs with their Muslim friends and neighbors. As a ministry, Crescent Project is committed to getting these packs into the hands of thousands of Muslims.

A Christian woman, upon hearing me speak on the radio about the Outreach Packs, called our office, and by faith, ordered ten, not sure to whom she would give them.

In addition to praying for some Muslim friends, she had specifically been praying for the leaders of the new mosque that was just built next door. She crossed the street to the mosque and welcomed the Imam (Muslim religious leader) to the neighborhood. Little could she have imagined when she ordered the Outreach Packs that she would be giving one to an Imam as a gift!

It is a joy to minister to Christ by faith, trusting Him to lead. He will water the seed and will be the one to draw people to Himself. We are to share the wonderful story of Jesus Christ, the Savior of the universe.

Visit a Muslim hairstylist or barber.
Ask questions about his or her life and family while getting your hair cut.

Join a community sports team.
Some parks and community centers organize soccer teams that could interest Muslim soccer players. Enjoy an active sport and make a Muslim friend.

Go prayerwalking.
Prayerwalk in a part of town where you know Muslims are located (maybe nearby a mosque or in your neighborhood). Pray for opportunities to meet Muslims on your walk.

———— Characterized by Compassion ————

"When He saw the crowds, He had compassion on them." (Matt. 9:36)

Most Muslims today have not experienced the compassion of Christ through believers' actions of friendship and service. The need of the hour is for Christians to relate to Muslims with compassion. A first step is demonstrating friendship by befriending a Muslim co-worker or greeting Muslims in your neighborhood. What might this look like? Jesus shows us the way.

Jesus took the initiative, modeling compassion and service. He left Heaven to be with and serve humanity (see Phil. 2:5-11). Motivated by his compassion for us, God took the initiative and reached out to us with a message of love, hope, and salvation.

Just as Jesus had compassion for men and women, God gives us compassion to motivate us to identify with, give aid, and show mercy to others. Let us ask God to give us this attitude of love and service, so we may continue our friendships with the Muslims God has placed around us.

Go to a bookstore.
Browse materials at an Islamic bookstore or the religion section of your local bookstore. It just might be that a Muslim employee or customer will browse beside you, ask you a question, or offer to help.

Strike up a conversation.
You can make small talk in the check-out line or sit beside a Muslim on a bench and "people watch" together. Introduce yourself and let God lead you from there.

Step 2: Initiating a Relationship

──────── Take the Initiative ────────

Once I sat by a Lebanese student on a flight from Beirut to Istanbul. As we put on our seatbelts, I knew he wasn't going anywhere! So I prayed, "Father, I am ready to share. Please open the door." God responded big time. Before we landed in Istanbul, this young man had decided to follow Christ!

When we work with Muslims, see them in shops, or sit next to them on airplanes, we should not wait for them to take the initiative to start a conversation or friendship. We should take the first step.

Whenever you meet a Muslim, pray silently, "Lord Jesus, I am ready to share about you. Please open the door for discussion." Christ will provide an entry!

Befriend the parents of your children's classmates.
By getting to know the parents of Muslim students at your child's school, natural opportunities for friendship abound when you can smile, ask a question about their child, or share a story about your own.

Be a host family for international students.
Often new international students, some of them Muslim, will be looking for a host family or language partner.

Set up a book table.
On a college campus, give out free Muslim-friendly materials, such as Bibles and the "JESUS" film. (Be sure to give out a multi-language version.) Curious Muslims may want to know why you are hosting the book table and your honest and friendly answer could initiate a lasting friendship. (For outreach materials, see the back of this booklet.)

Invite a Muslim acquaintance to join one of your groups.
It could be a book club, hiking club, sports team, or even an informal gathering of friends. Or instead, you may find a Muslim group you can join. Time spent together, especially when discussing different topics and issues, can deepen your friendship.

———— A Hunger for Connection ————

When Doug moved to a new community, he immediately began looking for Muslims playing soccer. Using his enjoyment for soccer seemed like a natural bridge to finding Muslims friends.

Driving up to a park not too far from the local mosque, Doug saw about 15 men playing soccer. His hopes were confirmed when he heard Arabic being called out across the field to teammates.

Since he didn't have his soccer gear with him, he sat and watched for a while. One player hurt his leg, so he came to the sideline – this was Doug's chance!

Doug went and introduced himself to the young man and found out that Abdul was a student at a nearby university. Doug asked, "So what brings you guys out here to play?"

Abdul looked at Doug almost apologetically. "We're all part of a Muslim community." As soon as he finished, he pulled back slightly, almost seeming to communicate, "OK, now's the time when you can run."

Doug responded, "Great. I'd love to join you."

Abdul was happily surprised and eagerly invited Doug to join them anytime.

It is unfortunate that a westerner wanting to play soccer with a group of Muslims should be so shocking.

Many Muslims have a desire for real connections, but sadly the church hasn't been reaching out. It's time to step out in faith that God will provide that friendship that both of you are looking for.

Be a faithful customer.
If you find a gas station operated by Muslims, be a "faithful customer" and fill up your tank there every time. Go inside to pay and interact with the attendant.

Invite Muslims to your home.
Be hospitable to your friend by providing drinks and snacks at the beginning of the visit and possibly tea or coffee near the end.

Give a Bible or other literature.
New Testaments can be great gifts. You can give a parallel New Testament to your friend so she can read about Jesus both in English and in her own language.

Baklava

On a Crescent Project mission trip to Beirut, Lebanon, the team entered a baklava store to try the delicious array of sweets. Asser, the owner of the store, began a conversation with Steve, one of our team members. Asser asked if all the team members were Evangelicals, to which he answered yes.

Asser immediately replied, "The Injeel (New Testament) has been changed." Steve said, "That's impossible! Who is stronger, God or the Christians?" Asser answered, "God is stronger."

Steve was expecting that response, so he replied, "If God is stronger, then God's word in the Injeel cannot be changed!"

To prove that the Injeel has been corrupted, Asser said, "The Injeel says that Jesus died on the cross." (The Qur'an teaches that Jesus did not die on the cross, so to many Muslims, this is one "proof" that the Bible has been changed.)

So Steve asked, "What glorifies God more, to help Jesus escape death? Or to help Jesus conquer death?" Asser responded that there are many things that glorify God.

Steve replied, "Yes, but the resurrection of Jesus proves that He was the Word of God in the flesh and proves that there is a resurrection. All religious leaders and prophets have died, but only Jesus rose from the dead as He said He would."

Asser was moved to ask if the team had an Arabic Injeel and if he could be in email contact with Steve. He said that he had never heard this about the Christian faith. Before leaving the store, the team also gave him a copy of my book, *Is the Injeel Corrupted?*

Pray for Asser, and consider pursuing training with Crescent Project, either at the Sahara Challenge or through the BRIDGES DVD Study. Join us in equipping yourself and your church in effectively communicating the Gospel to Muslims.

(For more information about training opportunities, as well as Bibles and other resources, visit www.crescentproject.org.)

Step 3: Deepening the Friendship

Plan a dinner for your Muslim and Christian friends.
Often Muslims will bring a dish to contribute, even if they're not asked. Steer clear of pork products, alcohol, and gelatin because these are considered unclean and sinful in Islam.

Visit your Muslim friend in his or her home.
Some Muslims feel greatly honored when you come to their home and benefit from their hospitality. If you come for a visit, call ahead, and plan to stay for at least an hour.

Try learning greetings and words in your friend's native language.
Starting with "hello" and "goodbye" in languages such as Arabic, Urdu, or Malay isn't as hard as you would think. (Note: In learning Arabic, don't recite the Islamic creed. This statement, known as the Shahada, is what someone recites to become a Muslim.)

Get a cooking lesson from your Muslim friend.
Go shopping together for ingredients and make the food in the home in which your friend feels most comfortable.

Take a trip together to a historical site or event in another community.
If your Muslim friends share your interest in sports, invite them to a game. Don't be afraid of a long road trip to visit Niagara Falls or the Grand Canyon: time together in the car will be valuable and your relationship will deepen considerably.

Pack a picnic lunch and share it at the park.
Everyone loves going to the park on a sunny day. You might be surprised at how good your conversations can be over a long game of croquet.

Go camping.
Pack a tent and an overnight bag and introduce your Muslim friend to an overnight camping trip in the wilderness.

Invite your friend to a holiday meal.
Ask your friends to join you for a family gathering or a weekend retreat with other Christians to celebrate the holidays, like Thanksgiving or Christmas. International students and immigrants will be especially surprised and delighted to celebrate the holiday with you! Share the spiritual significance of the holiday, and your friend will enjoy learning about your culture and religion.

Discuss current topics.
Your friend might be wondering about health care, education, or other issues. He or she may have questions about getting adequate health insurance or enrolling a child in a special reading program.

Attend a thought provoking movie together.
After the movie, have coffee together and discuss your impressions of the film and whether you agreed or disagreed with certain aspects of it. You can emphasize the Biblical principles that were portrayed.

Engage in conversation about moral issues.
These may include the sanctity of marriage ("How do you define marriage?"), abortion ("What is your stance on abortion?"), human rights issues ("Do you know the candidate's opinion on human rights issues?"), and others. You may find that you have more in common with your Muslim friend than you thought. Use election times as a good opening for this type of discussion.

Watch the "JESUS" film together.
Afterward, ask your friend if she has questions about what she saw. Maybe a question will come up half-way through. In this case, pause the video and answer it to the best of your knowledge. Point to Scripture when applicable, and show her the exact place in the Gospel where the scene from the movie originates.

It's All About Jesus!

Susan was visiting an apartment complex where most of the residents were Muslim. She met an Iraqi couple. Although they spoke very little English, they still somehow managed to communicate enough to discuss Jesus.

Susan asked if she could bring a copy of the "JESUS" film, and she was invited back the following day.

When Susan arrived, the wife greeted her and they sat down to watch the "JESUS" film. Unfortunately, she couldn't find her remote control, so they were unable to change the language track on the film. It wasn't English or Arabic, but they started to watch the movie anyway.

Susan remembered that she had a parallel Arabic-English New Testament in her car, so she went out to get it. So for the entire movie, Susan showed the Iraqi woman the verses in the Bible that corresponded to the scene in the movie.

After the movie, Susan walked through the Roman Road in the parallel New Testament. The Iraqi woman focused on Romans 10:9-10, and said in her broken English, "This me."

Just to make sure of what was happening, Susan called an Iraqi Christian friend on her phone. The two women spent time talking together and Susan's friend confirmed it – the Muslim woman had just chosen to follow Christ!

The "JESUS" film shown in an unknown language to an English speaking Christian helping an Arabic speaking Muslim read along in an Arabic-English Bible – it almost seems too comical to believe.

Don't underestimate the power of the life of Jesus, in film and in Scriptures. As your Muslim friends learn who the Jesus of the Bible is, they will be forced to realize that He isn't who they thought he was.

Attend an Islamic or cultural event.
Go to an Arab-American festival, a Persian film festival, or an Eid-ul-Fitr end of Ramadan celebration at a mosque. These events can be an excellent learning experience, and provide a topic for conversations later. "Do you have any other films from your country that I could see?" "What does the Ramadan fast mean to you?"

Go out for coffee and share cultural stories.
Don't be afraid to confess your ignorance, because your questions will show interest and identify common ground. "In what city were you born? For what things is your homeland known? What brought you to this country?"

Pray for them.
Asking Muslims how you can pray for them is a great way to learn their fears and concerns. Don't just say you'll pray—ask if you can pray right there! Pray from your heart and ask God to supply their needs. Then do all you can to be an answer to their prayers.

Step 4: Meeting Felt Needs of Muslims

—————— Physical Needs of Muslims ——————

On my first visit to an Iranian restaurant, I discovered that the owner's wife was sick. When I asked if I might pray for her physical healing, the man was grateful.

I explained that I would be asking in the name of Jesus, and he responded, "I believe Jesus is the healer." The Lord answered my prayers by healing the owner's wife. One week later, I was able to give him a New Testament.

We should pray for the Muslims in our community. If we know their names, we may pray daily for them and ask the Lord to make "divine appointments." We will be pleasantly surprised as the Lord orchestrates events for us to be witnesses.

International Students and Immigrants

Be an English conversation partner.
Some libraries and universities have programs to help non-native speakers of English hone their language skills. Why not help tutor an international student, or start your own ESL course in your church or community? Post an advertisement in apartment complexes where Muslim immigrants live or in ethnic stores and restaurants.

Assist with immigration issues.
Muslims often must sift through complicated papers and attend various court dates involving their visa and immigration status. Ask if you can help drive him to an appointment or help explain the paperwork. Also, check with a local relief group or immigration office to see if they need help resettling refugees from Muslim countries. The service you offer will make your country seem more inviting and make their transition easier.

Host an international fair for college students.
Have students set up a table about their country, make their ethnic dishes, and dress in their traditional clothing.

Have a student over for dinner.
Once a month, host an international Muslim student in your home. Learn more about his life, classes, and friends, and seek to be his "home away from home."

Transport students to appointments and meetings.
Taking internationals to doctor's appointments can greatly decrease their anxiety about living in a foreign country.

Show a Muslim student where to shop.
Introduce students to the process of going to a grocery store, to places like Target or Wal-Mart, and to the drive-through at a bank.

Ride the bus together.
You can show a Muslim student how to use the public transit system in your city by finding the routes and stop times online and riding the system with him the first time.

Introduce new cultural activities.
Your friend may not have attended a baseball game, amusement park, St. Patrick's Day parade, or theater performance. Historical sites in your city might also provide the opportunity to educate the newcomer to local history.

Women

Be a driving coach.
Teaching your Muslim friend to drive and helping her get her license can greatly increase her freedom. It might be a nerve-wracking experience, so help her learn in a deserted area (like a parking lot and open streets) and pray to demonstrate patience and love.

Host a baby shower for expectant mothers.
Your Muslim friend may not want the attention directed to her, so make the celebration one of games and food, while downplaying the importance of gifts.

Join a gym exclusively for women.
Your friends may be more comfortable working out in a ladies-only gym. Schedule "tea time" after workouts for further interaction.

Give a gift that has meaning.
Gifts of perfume, lotions, or bath salts can be an opportunity to share about the fragrance of our lives to God. Other gifts like baked goods can bear an attached note that includes a verse of Scripture about God's faithfulness or some other theme.

Provide an environment to be in the sun.
When Muslim women cover, sometimes they are unable to get enough Vitamin D from sun exposure, which has resulted in outbreaks of Rickets. This can be solved by simply spending time outdoors on sunny days. Try walking, playing tennis, taking the kids to the neighborhood pool, or participating in other leisure activities.

Sew, knit, or quilt together.
Finding simple activities like this where you can learn and participate together can open up long stretches of time for conversation, and with the focus being on the "activity," the conversation may flow more freely.

Host a cosmetics party.
Get facials together with your friends and enjoy the freedom of just being with a group of women. Kitchen parties like Pampered Chef and jewelry parties are also popular. Be sure the consultant is willing to help you create an environment for friendships to grow.

Throw a henna party.
Some Muslim women enjoy decorating each other's arms with henna designs for special events. Host a women-only evening where every woman can have henna done without going to a salon!

Families

Offer after-school tutoring.
Are you skilled in subjects like math or language arts? Tutoring or providing music lessons can be a great way to befriend an entire Muslim family by investing in their child's education.

Invite them to your child's birthday party.
If your child has a Muslim classmate, invite them to a party. Call the parent and explain what will be happening at the event. Ask if he or she would like to be present and help with the setup.

Provide good, clean fun.
Muslim parents can struggle with allowing their children to mix with non-Muslims, fearing they may be poorly influenced. Church youth group events, movie nights, and game nights can provide a safe environment for Muslim parents to send their kids.

Invite parents to join you in the Parent-Teacher Association.
Your relationship can grow as you share in being involved in your children's school activities.

Worldview

Because you and your friend have a different religious and cultural background, your worldviews will be different. Simply put, a worldview is the way an individual or group looks at the universe.

Your friend may do or say something that seems contrary to what you had expected. Perhaps you are looking at their action through your own worldview, but in his or her context, that action made sense.

How can you discover your friend's worldview? Ask many questions. This will help to show you where your friend is coming from and lead towards a deeper relationship. Good questions can help you understand not just worldview, but also feelings, needs, and aspirations—touching the heart, and not just the mind. And as you get to know your Muslim friend on a deeper level, won't this help you as you share Christ?

Step 5: Asking Good Questions

In your conversations, ask questions about your Muslim friend's life, culture, family, history, festivals, likes and dislikes. This is the only way to find out what he or she believes. Don't assume anything...ask!

- What country are you from?
- How long have you been in this country?
- Can you tell me about where you are from?
- What is the best thing about your country?
- What did you like and dislike about growing up there?
- What do you like about this country?
- What did you like about being raised a Muslim?
- What was your most difficult experience as a child?
- Did you know any Christians growing up? What was your opinion of them?
- How do you practice your religion? Which practices mean the most to you personally?
- What holidays (or Eids) do you participate in?
- Why do you think there are different religions?
- Who is Jesus, in your opinion? How did you learn this about Jesus?
- What have you heard about Jesus? How do you know those facts are true?
- Have you read the Injeel (New Testament), which is the revelation given to Jesus?

The Five Pillars of Christianity

Often Muslims are left confused by the varying denominations and sects within Christianity. Emphasize that there are 5 Pillars that every follower of Jesus believes and show them the corresponding Scriptures. They are:

- **One God** – Christians believe in one God.
  (1 Corinthians 8:5-6)

- **One Savior** – Christians believe in one Savior who offers redemption to all people.
  (2 Timothy 1:10)

- **One Spirit** – Christians are filled and empowered by one Spirit.
  (Acts 1:8)

- **One Message** – Christians are unified by one message.
  (Mark 1:14-15)

- **One Family** – Christians are part of one family.
  (Galatians 3:28; John 1:12)

Step 6: Sharing Your Faith

Create a friendly environment.
It is within the context of friendly interaction that the Good News can be shared easily and naturally. Let your friend see Christ in your actions, attitudes, and daily struggles. Whether with an acquaintance, classmate, coworker, or neighbor, the environment you create in your discussions should be friendly and open for sharing and dialog.

Discuss religious issues.
In our culture, we're often told to avoid talking about religion. However, because religion is so intricately woven into the life of the Muslim, this is usually a safe topic. Ask questions about your friend's religion, and then use their responses to build bridges to Christ.

Be sensitive to your friend's responses.
If he or she seems unwilling to answer a question you have posed, maybe it is too invasive a question for this stage in the relationship. Simply move on or share a story of your own.

Use common issues as a bridge to the Gospel.
Keep communication open by discussing issues that you have in common, not those that divide. Agree whenever possible, especially with anything consistent with the Bible.

Listen.
A good listener focuses on the friend's concerns and needs. Look for bridges between his or her understanding and biblical truths.

Maintain a consistent lifestyle.
Live so that your friend can see the difference between you and the culture around you. The Gospel of Christ is the power of God for salvation from sin and deliverance from sin's power.

—————— "Follower of Christ" ——————

When Muslims live in what is considered a "Christian country," they may think that everything in that culture is a reflection and result of Christianity.

If Muslims believe that the values of Hollywood, Brittney Spears, and "Desperate Housewives" represent what Christianity is about, then there is a crisis of information.

Who among us would desire Christ if following Him meant promiscuity, broken families, and selfishness? When we share the Gospel, some Muslims may think that this is what they are being invited into!

As followers of Christ, we must live our lives in such a way that we stand in stark contrast to the morals and lifestyles that entertainment and the media love to portray.

Chris was visiting a mosque on "Community Day" and had the chance to talk with Sameer, a Muslim in his 50s who clearly had lived in North America for decades – his native accent was very subtle.

Chris began a sentence, "Well, as a follower of Christ, I..." but was cut off by Sameer before he could finish.

"Follower of Christ? What does that mean?" Sameer asked.

Chris explained. "Many people call themselves Christians just because their parents were Christian or they were born in this country. But as a Follower of Christ, my relationship with God is very important to me, and my desire is to live a life based upon the Bible and the life of Christ."

Tragically, Sameer responded, "I've never heard this before!"

We think that when we share the Good News of Jesus Christ, people will be attracted to the words we say. Unfortunately, for some, their negative associations, even if wrong, have raised up barriers.

Through holy living and patient sharing, you can help your friends to lower their barriers to the Gospel and see what they are truly being invited into – a personal relationship with the Living God!

Share your testimony.
Tell how God transformed your life through the power of the Gospel. When you share, include what your life was like before you met God, how you met Him, and how your life has changed since knowing God.

Pray regularly for your friend.
Pray that God will reveal your friend's needs to you, and that the Holy Spirit will intervene supernaturally in his or her life. Your words are just one part of God's intervention.

Be discerning with non-practicing Muslims.
If your friend is a "cultural" Muslim and doesn't practice Islam, reach out to them like you would other non-Christians. Talk with him about his need for peace, how he handles stress in his life, and where his hope comes from.

Be in it for the long haul.
Many Muslims come from cultures that view friendship very differently than in the West. Once you've crossed from acquaintances to friends, the expectation is that you'll be involved in their lives. It's a commitment to befriend Muslims, but the blessing is worth it.

Relax! Don't panic! God is on the throne!
It is not your job to "convert" your Muslim friend but to share your faith and pray for God to work in his or her life.

Be observant of your Muslim friend's customs.
Notice how she sits or eats, or how he enters a house. Even how we treat our Bibles (putting them on the floor, or stacking other things on top of them) communicates disrespect. Our cultural habits may be an affront to their sensibilities.

Interact men with men, women with women.
Men and women are usually separated in Islam, and piety and purity respected (as they are in Christianity). Women, always dress modestly and do not enter a gathering of all men. Men, do not enter a home where no other men are present.

Side step debate or argument.
Let winning your friend to Christ be your goal, not winning the argument. Our message is not about religion, its regimen or rituals, or a philosophical system; it is about a relationship with God through Jesus Christ. Express your gratitude for what he has done for you.

Avoid insulting the Qur'an, Muhammad, or Islam.
Humiliation is alienating, but our description of Jesus and his work is appealing and will draw our friend closer to faith.

The Glory of the Son

In the morning, what happens to the stars when the sun comes up? Do the stars go anywhere? No, but as the sun rises and its brightness fills the sky, the stars simply fade away.

The same is true as we lift up Jesus Christ. We don't need to tear down Islam, and speaking negatively of Muhammad won't bring greater openness in discussions. We simply point our friend to Christ. The shining glory of the Son can simply make all other things fade away.

Be a good, loving friend.
Your unconditional love will attract him or her to our best friend, Jesus Christ, in whose hands are the results.

Christians should not criticize one another.
Refrain from putting down other Christians, denominations, or ministries. Even though some Christian leaders have been negative towards Islam and Muslims, we must remain positive as we interact with our Muslim friend. You can explain that in Christianity, people are allowed to share their opinions freely. However, always bring the focus back to the Biblical teachings of Christ and not controversies.

Share about Christ as the sacrifice, or true Adha.
Eid al-Adha is an excellent opportunity to learn about the Muslim holiday and share about the "Christian Adha." Ultimately, our message to our Muslim friends needs to be about Jesus!

—— Eid al-Adha: The Feast of Sacrifice ——

Every year Muslims around the world celebrate the feast of *Eid al-Adha*, also known as the Feast of Sacrifice or Great Feast (*Eid ul-Kabir*), in Southeast Asia as *Bakr Eid*, and in the Turkic world as *Kurban Bayram*. At this time, many Muslims sacrifice a sheep or goat to commemorate how God redeemed the son of Abraham, as recorded in the Qur'an (Sura 37:99-113). Jews also preserve the meaning of this event through the Passover celebration.

But where is the Christian sacrifice? Since Christians believe in both the Abrahamic sacrifice and the Passover, why don't they celebrate them?

Just as God redeemed the son of Abraham with the sacrifice he provided in a ram, so God redeemed the world through the blood of Jesus Christ. Jesus became the true *Adha*: he was the Lamb of God, sacrificed to set us free from sin, by which God bridged the gulf that separated us from Him. So Christians do have a sacrifice: the once-for-all sacrifice of Jesus Christ, which we celebrate every Easter!

Go for It!

Seven million Muslims in North America are still looking for an authentic Christian witness. You have a Hope worth sharing.

We are called to faithfully love people and share Christ, then we leave the results up to God. I pray with you as you step out in faith to love and build relationships with Muslims.

I'd love to hear your stories. If you have a testimony of how this booklet was helpful, or if we can answer any questions, please contact us at www.crescentproject.org or info@crescentproject.org.

So go for it! As we obey Christ's call to reach the nations, let us rejoice that He brought the "nations" into our neighborhoods.

"May the God of peace, who through the blood of the eternal covenant brought back from the dead our Lord Jesus, that great Shepherd of the sheep, equip you with everything good for doing his will, and may he work in us what is pleasing to Him, through Jesus Christ, to whom be glory for ever and ever. Amen."
Hebrews 13:20-21

crescent project

HOPE WORTH SHARING

We welcome your inquiries at:

Crescent Project
P.O. Box 50986 • Indianapolis, IN 46250 • USA

www.crescentproject.org
info@crescentproject.org

BRIDGES

The BRIDGES curriculum was developed by Crescent Project to introduce you and your church to Islam and pave the way for building relationships with the Muslims in your community.

This 6-session DVD Small Group Study provides Biblical teaching about Islam and what Muslims believe, opening the door for you to more effectively share your faith.

www.crescentproject.org/bridgesdvd

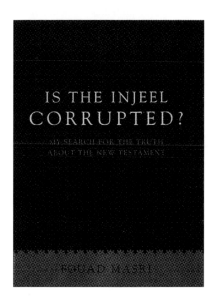

Is the Injeel Corrupted?

Both Muslims and Christians honor the Injeel, or New Testament. However, most Muslims view the Book of Jesus as unreliable and unimportant to read and obey.

"Is the Injeel Corrupted?" tackles a critical question for skeptical Muslims and Christians who are eager to present truth.

By addressing the theological, logical, and historical proofs for the New Testament's credibility, Fouad Masri's 65-page book answers these questions in a way that is relevant to the Muslim heart and mind.

www.crescentproject.org/istheinjeel

Adha in the Injeel

Muslims around the world annually celebrate the feast of Al-Adha, which is is also known as the "Feast of Sacrifice". At the Al-Adha feast, many Muslims sacrifice a sheep or a ram to commemorate the holy event when God redeemed the son of Abraham by providing a ram caught in the thicket for the sacrifice.

"Adha in the Injeel" is a booklet written for Muslims explaining salvation through Christ's death and resurrection by using the Islamic story of the Adha as an illustration of how Christ is our Adha.

www.crescentproject.org/adha

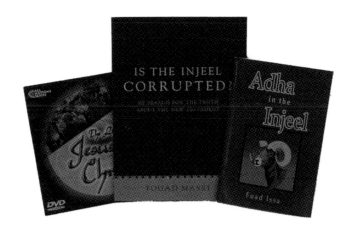

Outreach Pack

Share the Good News of Jesus with a Muslim friend or neighbor! This gift pack addresses many of the common questions Muslims typically have about Jesus and the Bible.

This pack includes:

- Is the Injeel Corrupted?
- Adha in the Injeel
- The "JESUS" Film (in 16 languages)

Discounts available for bulk purchases.

www.crescentproject.org/outreachpack